EARLY JAZZ AND SWING SONGS FOR GUITAR

by DAVID HAMBURGER

Editor: Jeffrey Pepper Rodgers

Author photograph: Stephen Hunt

ISBN 978-0-634-08775-2

STRING LETTER PUBLISHING

EXCLUSIVELY DISTRIBUTED BY

HAL•LEONARD® CORPORATION

7777 W. BLUEMOUND RD. P.O. BOX 13819 MILWAUKEE, WI 53213

Visit Hal Leonard Online at
www.halleonard.com

In Australia Contact:
Hal Leonard Australia Pty. Ltd.
22 Taunton Drive P.O. Box 5130
Cheltenham East, 3192 Victoria, Australia
Email: ausadmin@halleonard.com

CONTENTS

INTRODUCTION

Early jazz refers to a period in American popular music that lasted from the late 'teens through the 1920s; the swing era basically refers to the 1930s. These periods overlap, of course, since musicians from the '20s continued playing throughout the 1930s and beyond, and the swing players of the '30s likewise continued to perform and record into the subsequent decades.

With one exception, the 15 songs in this book were composed by professional songwriters in the first quarter of the 20th century. They were written as popular songs, to be sung in theatrical shows and revues and to be sold as sheet music, which at the time was still a bigger business than the sale of recordings. By the mid-1920s, as Louis Armstrong was hitting his stride with his Hot Five and Hot Seven sessions, recorded music was having its first big boom, and the interpretations of jazz musicians like Armstrong began to create a whole second life for certain popular songs. Jazz groups recorded these tunes with looser, more swinging interpretations of the melodies, new chord voicings, and a jazz pulse, generally using the songs as vehicles for improvisation. This fresh approach served to pull the songs in this book into what was then just becoming the jazz repertoire.

By the 1930s the swing orchestras of Fletcher Henderson, Count Basie, and Benny Goodman were streamlining and refining the innovations made by Armstrong, Jelly Roll Morton, and others. Having cut their teeth on the music of the 1920s, Henderson, Basie, Goodman, and their peers and sidemen naturally gravitated toward reinterpreting those tunes, even as they composed new pieces and chose current show music to arrange. So we get Basie's and Goodman's versions of "Royal Garden Blues," Goodman's and Henderson's versions of "Rose Room," Basie's and Fats Waller's versions of "I Ain't Got Nobody," Goodman's and Jimmy Lunceford's versions of "Avalon"—all songs written a good 15 to 20 years before and given new life in the latest popular style.

History exerts a winnowing effect on the music of the past—the 1960s' reputation as a golden era of rock 'n' roll, for instance, rests as much on forgetting the work of the Archies as on remembering that of Beatles and Bob Dylan. With the jazz age, too, certain songs have emerged as standards while countless other topical, novelty, and sentimental songs lie crumbling in the dust where they probably belong. In terms of the jazz repertoire, a standard is simply a song still in circulation because at some point an artist with sufficient influence saw fit to treat it as jazz material, and enough others subsequently ratified that first musician's judgement by recording and performing the song themselves.

Early Jazz and Swing Songs includes the melody and chords to 15 standards in the public domain. The CD includes a two-guitar recording of each arrangement, but to really learn how to play these tunes, especially the melodies, I suggest tracking down at least one original recording of each song. I have stayed close to the published sheet-music versions of the melodies found in Hal Leonard's *Early Jazz Standards*, and more than a few of the tunes sound somewhat square when played that way. I did so, however, because even by the 1930s, many jazz musicians' renditions of these tunes were loose interpretations of the original theme, and if you want to understand the kind of improvisors they were, there are few better places to start than observing how they ornamented and re-created the melodies.

I hope you have fun learning to play these tunes. Like fiddle tunes or classic rock songs, early jazz and swing standards are a great meeting ground for casual jamming with friends and fellow musicians. So once you've got a few of these under your fingers, don't hesitate to try them out the next time you're doing some picking. Good luck!

Introduction and Tune-Up:

Need help with the songs in this book? Ask a question in our free, on-line support forum in the Guitar Talk section of www.acousticguitar.com.

THE RHYTHM STYLE

I've arranged the chord progressions in this book in what guitarists call the Freddie Green style, after the rhythm guitarist who reportedly took only one recorded solo in his five decades with the Count Basie orchestra. While such nobility may not be your cup of Darjeeling, Green nevertheless perfected a comping (as in, ac-*comp*-animent) style that lays down just the right groove for a swing interpretation of the melody. There are two components to this style: what chords to play and how to play them. Let's look at each one before we get into the tunes themselves.

THE CHORDS

Jazz guitarists tend to use four-note chord voicings, but Green's style trimmed each chord down to the three notes found on the sixth, fourth, and third strings, as shown below in the second row. (Note that there is no commonly used four-note version of the G/D, so just the three-note version is shown.) You can play all 15 arrangements in this book using just these nine chord shapes.

TRACK 2

Four-Note Voicings

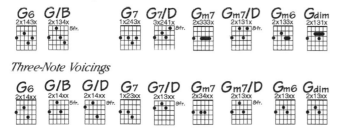

Several of these chords have the third or the fifth of the chord on the lowest string, rather than the root. You may also have noticed that the Gm6, G7/D, and Gdim chords all have the exact same shape. These chords are meant to be played with a bassist, who is presumably playing the root of the chord on the first beat of each measure. Heard out of that context, these chords may not sound right at first, which is another good reason to spend some time with original recordings of these tunes and even to try and play along with them.

Wherever possible, I've arranged these songs in the keys in which they were first published. While jazz musicians usually stick to the original key, sometimes another key becomes a popular alternative—for example, "Indiana" is just as frequently played in the key of F as in the original key of Ab. And standards are frequently moved to another key to accommodate a vocalist.

STRUMMING

In the swing era, the guitarist was usually part of a four-piece rhythm section that also included piano, bass, and drums. Keeping good time meant providing a steady flow of quarter notes, four per bar, by playing a downstroke on every beat and possibly emphasizing beats 2 and 4 somewhat. If you let your fretting fingers mute the fifth, second, and first strings, you can do a big, percussive strum across all six strings and just hear the notes you want to hear, on the sixth, fourth, and third strings. Relaxing your grip at the end of each quarter note dampens the strings and creates a little space between each stroke.

At slower tempos, the four strums in a bar tend to come out relatively evenly, as in Example 1. At a moderate tempo (Example 2), the second and fourth beats start to get more clipped. And at faster tempos (Example 3), the second and fourth beats tend to become just a percussive backbeat.

TRACK 3

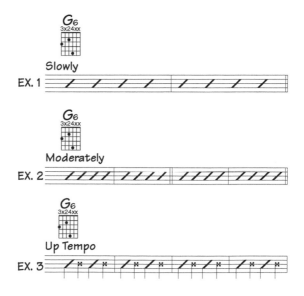

MUSIC NOTATION KEY

The music in this book is written in standard notation and tablature. Here's how to read it.

STANDARD NOTATION

Standard notation is written on a five-line staff. Notes are written in alphabetical order from A to G.

The duration of a note is determined by three things: the note head, stem, and flag. A whole note (o) equals four beats. A half note (♩) is half of that: two beats. A quarter note (♩) equals one beat, an eighth note (♪) equals half of one beat, and a 16th note (♬) is a quarter beat (there are four 16th notes per beat).

The fraction (4/4, 3/4, 6/8, etc.) or c character shown at the beginning of a piece of music denotes the time signature. The top number tells you how many beats are in each measure, and the bottom number indicates the rhythmic value of each beat (4 equals a quarter note, 8 equals an eighth note, 16 equals a 16th note, and 2 equals a half note). The most common time signature is 4/4, which signifies four quarter notes per measure and is sometimes designated with the symbol c (for common time). The symbol ¢ stands for cut time (2/2). Most songs are either in 4/4 or 3/4.

TABLATURE

In tablature, the six horizontal lines represent the six strings of the guitar, with the first string on the top and sixth on the bottom. The numbers refer to fret numbers on a given string. The notation and tablature in this book are designed to be used in tandem—refer to the notation to get the rhythmic information and note durations, and refer to the tablature to get the exact locations of the notes on the guitar fingerboard.

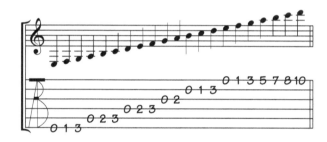

CHORD DIAGRAMS

Chord diagrams show where the fingers go on the fingerboard. Frets are shown horizontally, and the thick top line represents the nut. The sixth (lowest-pitched) string is on the far left, and first (highest-pitched) string is on the far right. Dots show where the fingers go, and the numbers above the diagram tell you which fretting-hand fingers to use: 1 for the index finger, 2 the middle, 3 the ring, 4 the fourth finger, and *T* the thumb. An *X* indicates a string that should be muted or not played; 0 indicates an open string.

ARTICULATIONS

There are a number of ways you can articulate a note on the guitar. Notes connected with slurs (not to be confused with ties) in the tablature or standard notation are articulated with a hammer-on, a pull-off, or a slide. Lower notes slurred to higher notes are played as hammer-ons; higher notes slurred to lower notes are played as pull-offs. While it's usually obvious that slurred notes are played as hammer-ons or pull-offs, an *H* or *P* is included above the tablature as an extra reminder.

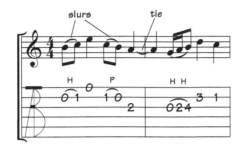

Slides are represented with a dash, and an *S* is included above the tab. A dash preceding a note represents a slide into the note from an indefinite point in the direction of the slide; a dash following a note indicates a slide off of the note to an indefinite point in the direction of the slide. For two slurred notes connected with a slide, you should pick the first note and then slide into the second.

Grace notes are represented by small notes with a dash through the stem in standard notation and with small numbers in the tab. A grace note is a very quick ornament leading into a note, most commonly executed as a hammer-on, pull-off, or slide. In the following example, pluck the note at the fifth fret on the beat, then quickly hammer onto the seventh fret. The second example is executed as a quick pull-off from the second fret to the open string. In the third example, both notes at the fifth fret are played simultaneously (even though it appears that the fifth fret, fourth string, is to be played by itself), then the seventh fret, fourth string, is quickly hammered.

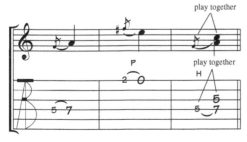

REPEATS

One of the most confusing parts of a musical score can be the navigation symbols, such as repeats, *D.S. al Coda*, *D.C. al Fine*, *To Coda*, etc.

Repeat symbols are placed at the beginning and end of the passage to be repeated.

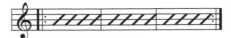

You should ignore repeat symbols with the dots on the right side the first time you encounter them; when you come to a repeat symbol with dots on the left side, jump back to the previous repeat symbol facing the opposite direction (if there is no previous symbol, go to the beginning of the piece). The next time you come to the repeat symbol, ignore it and keep going unless it includes instructions such as "Repeat three times."

Often a section has a different ending after each repeat. The example below includes a first and a second ending. Play until you hit the repeat symbol, jump back to the previous repeat symbol and play until you reach the bracketed first ending, skip the measures under the bracket and jump immediately to the second ending, and then continue.

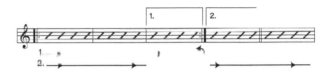

D.S. stands for *dal segno* or "from the sign." When you encounter this indication, jump immediately to the sign (𝄋). *D.S.* is usually accompanied by *al Fine* or *al Coda*. *Fine* indicates the end of a piece. A coda is a final passage near the end of a piece and is indicated with ⊕. *D.S. al Coda* simply tells you to jump back to the sign and continue on until you are instructed to jump to the coda, indicated with *To Coda* ⊕.

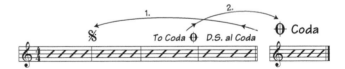

D.C. stands for *da capo* or "from the beginning." Jump to the top of the piece when you encounter this indication.

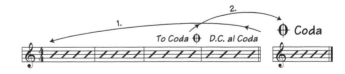

D.C. al Fine tells you to jump to the beginning of a tune and continue until you encounter the *Fine* indicating the end of the piece (ignore the *Fine* the first time through).

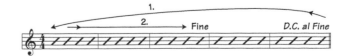

ST. JAMES INFIRMARY

Traditional

Folksinger Dave Van Ronk traces this tune, which he recorded as "Gambler's Blues" on his first Folkways record (*Folkways Years: 1959–1961*, Smithsonian Folkways 40041) back to a mid–19th-century Irish song called "The Unfortunate Rake." Trumpeter Louis Armstrong recorded it in the 1920s (*Louis Armstrong and His Orchestra: 1928–1929*, Classics 570), and it's been done by countless blues and jazz musicians ever since. The fingerstyle version I recorded on my *Barrelhouse Guitar* CD (Chester 0027) uses similar chord changes to those in Version 2.

Version 1 can be played using just one chord shape, making this a good place to start, even though the chords change every two beats except in measure 4. If the additional chord shapes in Version 2 throw you off (C6 in measures 2 and 6 and a Bm7 in measure 4), try revisiting this arrangement after you've gotten the next few songs under your belt.

I WENT DOWN TO OLD JOE'S BARROOM ON THE CORNER BY THE SQUARE
THEY WERE SERVING DRINKS AS USUAL, AND THE USUAL CROWD WAS THERE

ON MY LEFT STOOD BIG JOE MCKENNEDY, HIS EYES WERE BLOODSHOT RED
AND AS HE TURNED TO FACE THE CROWD THERE, THESE ARE THE VERY WORDS THAT HE SAID

I WENT DOWN TO THE SAINT JAMES INFIRMARY TO SEE MY BABY THERE
BUT SHE WAS LAID OUT ON THE MARBLE, SO SWEET, SO COLD, SO FAIR

LET HER GO, LET HER GO, GOD BLESS HER, WHEREVER SHE MAY BE
SHE CAN TRAVEL THE WIDE WORLD OVER AND NEVER FIND ANOTHER MAN LIKE ME

WHEN I DIE, WON'T YOU BURY ME IN MY HIGH-TOP STETSON HAT
PUT A TWENTY-DOLLAR GOLD PIECE ON MY WATCH CHAIN SO MY FRIENDS WILL KNOW I DIED STANDING PAT

I WANT SIX GAMBLERS TO BEAR MY COFFIN, SIX CHORUS GIRLS TO SING ME A SONG
PUT A TWENTY-PIECE JAZZ BAND ON MY TAILGATE, RAISING HELL AS I ROLL ALONG

NOW I'VE TOLD MY STORY, LET'S HAVE ANOTHER ROUND OF BOOZE
AND IF ANYONE SHOULD ASK YOU, I'VE GOT THE SAINT JAMES INFIRMARY BLUES

T'AIN'T NOBODY'S BUSINESS IF I DO

Words and music by Porter Grainger and Everett Robbins

Like "St. James Infirmary," "T'ain't Nobody's Business" is an eight-bar blues. Billie Holiday did one of the definitive versions (included on *Billie Holiday's Greatest Hits*, GRP 653), as did one of her great inspirations, blues diva Bessie Smith (*The Essential Bessie Smith*, Columbia/Legacy 64922).

Here's a tip for switching among the three chord shapes in Version 1: Bb6, D7, Eb7, and F7 all involve holding down the same shape on the sixth and fourth strings with your middle and index fingers. So to switch, say, from Bb6 to D7, just slide back one fret with your middle and index fingers; as you do so, lift your pinkie off the seventh fret of the third string and replace it with your ring finger on the

fifth fret of the same string. You can use a similar trick to get from F7 back to Bb6. You'll be sliding back two frets with your index and middle fingers, and this time, remove your ring finger from the eighth fret of the third string and replace it with your pinkie at the seventh fret.

Version 2 includes two new major chord shapes, the Eb in measure 4 and the Bb/D in measure 5. As with "St. James Infirmary," you may want to check back in with this version once you've worked through a few more of the following tunes. The Eb in particular is a bit of a stretch but will get easier the more you use it.

Version 1

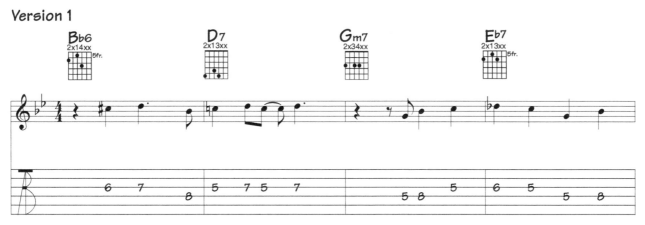

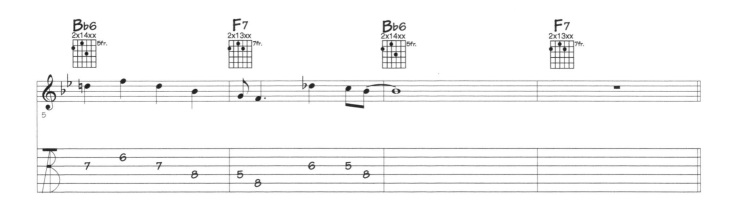

Version 2

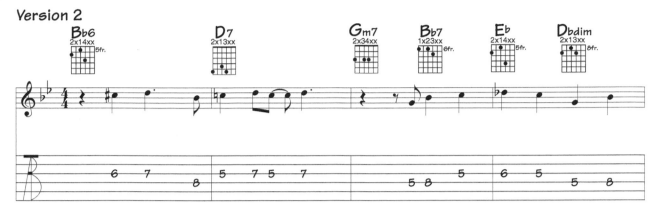

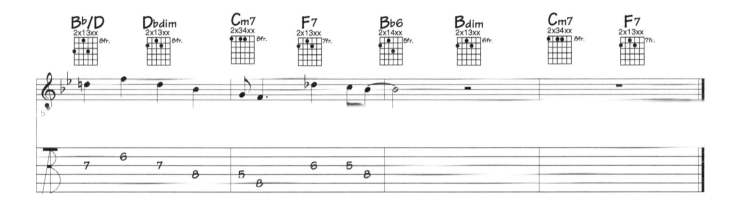

IF I SHOULD TAKE A NOTION TO JUMP INTO THE OCEAN
AIN'T NOBODY'S BUSINESS IF I DO

IF I GO TO CHURCH ON SUNDAY, THEN CABARET ON MONDAY
AIN'T NOBODY'S BUSINESS IF I DO

IF MY FRIEND AIN'T GOT NO MONEY, AND I SAY TAKE ALL OF MINE, HONEY
AIN'T NOBODY'S BUSINESS IF I DO

IF I GIVE HIM MY LAST NICKEL, AND IT LEAVES ME IN A PICKLE
AIN'T NOBODY'S BUSINESS IF I DO

IF I LET MY BEST COMPANION DRIVE ME RIGHT INTO THE CANYON
AIN'T NOBODY'S BUSINESS IF I DO

IF I DON'T LIKE MY LOVER AND LEAVE HIM FOR ANOTHER
AIN'T NOBODY'S BUSINESS IF I DO

ST. LOUIS BLUES

Words and music by W. C. Handy

If you're acquainted with the classic 12-bar blues form, you may find this tune at once familiar and surprising. That's because the first and third sections both follow a 12-bar blues form (though with different melodies) while the middle section changes from G major to G minor and lasts for 16 bars. Published by the African-American musician and composer W. C. Handy in 1914, the song has a middle section that was meant to be played with a tangolike Latin feel—what New Orleans jazz pianist Jelly Roll Morton famously referred to as "the Spanish tinge." Louis

Armstrong opened his version (Louis Armstrong, *Volume 6: St. Louis Blues*, Columbia/Legacy 46996) with the middle section, as did the guitar duo of Weaver and Beasley, though their slide guitar version (included on the compilation *The Slide Guitar: Bottles, Knives, and Steel*, Columbia/Legacy 46218) is in a slow two-beat feel. It's also possible to swing through all three sections, as Benny Goodman's band was doing by the 1930s (check out *The Very Best of Benny Goodman*, RCA 63730), so I've arranged it that way here.

I HATE TO SEE THE EVENING SUN *GO* DOWN
I HATE TO SEE THE EVENING SUN *GO* DOWN
SINCE MY BABY UP AND LEFT THIS TOWN

ST. LOUIS WOMAN WITH HER DIAMOND RINGS
PULLS THAT MAN AROUND BY HER APRON STRINGS
IF IT WEREN'T FOR POWDER AND FOR STORE-BOUGHT HAIR
THE MAN I LOVE WOULDN'T HAVE GONE NOWHERE

GOT THE ST. LOUIS BLUES, JUST AS BLUE AS I CAN BE
THAT MAN'S GOT A HEART LIKE A ROCK CAST INTO THE SEA
OR ELSE HE WOULDN'T HAVE GONE SO FAR FROM ME

ROYAL GARDEN BLUES

Music by Clarence Williams and Spencer Williams

Like "St. Louis Blues," "Royal Garden Blues" has three sections. This time all three sections follow the 12-bar blues pattern, but there are a few twists. The first section is played twice, following the melody both times. In the second section, also played twice, the repeated one-bar riff is usually passed around the band, with a different instrument playing the riff in each measure before a fourth musician solos over the remaining eight bars of the section.

I've composed a solo for you to try the first time around, and left a space on the recording for you to try a solo of your own the second time around. Next, there's a four-bar interlude that's played only once before the entire

song *modulates*, or changes keys, to B♭. The third section is a blues in B♭ that's just for soloing. On recordings by the Benny Goodman Sextet with Charlie Christian on guitar (Charlie Christian, *Genius of the Electric Guitar*, Columbia 40846), Count Basie (*America's #1 Band: The Columbia Years*, Columbia 87110), Bix Beiderbecke (*Volume 2: At the Jazz Band Ball*, Columbia/Legacy 46175), and others, once the band completes the interlude and starts the third section, they play the blues in B♭ with various soloists taking any number of improvised choruses until the end of the tune.

BALLIN' THE JACK

Words by Jim Burris, music by Chris Smith

Like most of the tunes in this book and many others that have become jazz standards, "Ballin' the Jack" has an opening section, called the verse, that sets up the story of the song, followed by the 16 bars below, originally called the refrain or chorus. The refrain is the part that everyone ultimately remembers and plays and that jazz musicians use as a vehicle for improvising, though it's considered the essence of cool for a musician to be aware of the verses to these kinds of tunes. You can hear one performance of "Ballin' the Jack" on Chet Atkins, *Guitar Legend: The RCA Years* (Buddha 99673). Jazz guitarist and bandleader Eddie Condon recorded a version on *Dr. Jazz: Volume 16* (Storyville 6061), although, like Freddie Green, Condon often left the dirty work of soloing to others.

"Ballin' the Jack" was the 1913 equivalent of "The Hustle" or "The Macarena," a dance tune about how to do said dance. As the verse states, "Play some good rag, that will make you prance / Old folks, young folks, all try to do the dance / Jump in now while you got the chance / Once again the steps to you I'll show...."

Family lore has it that this was my grandmother's favorite song, and while I have no idea what it means to do the Eagle Rock, with grace and style or otherwise, I like to picture her heading home with her girlfriends on the Culver train to Coney Island after a night of cabaret hijinks in which this tune figured heavily.

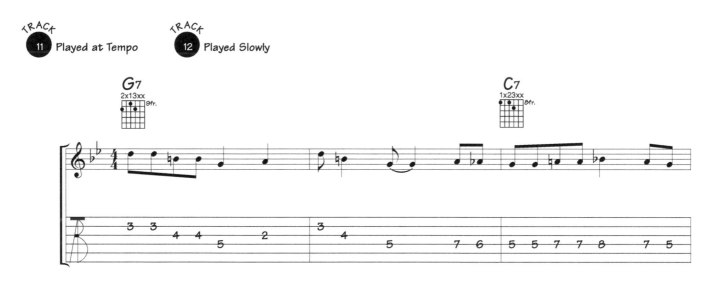

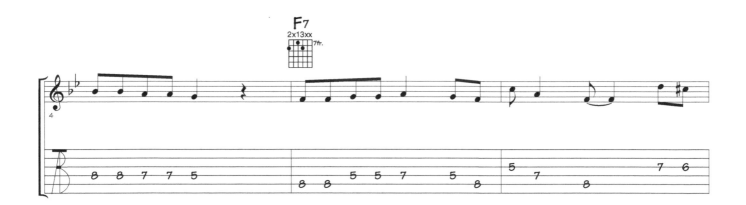

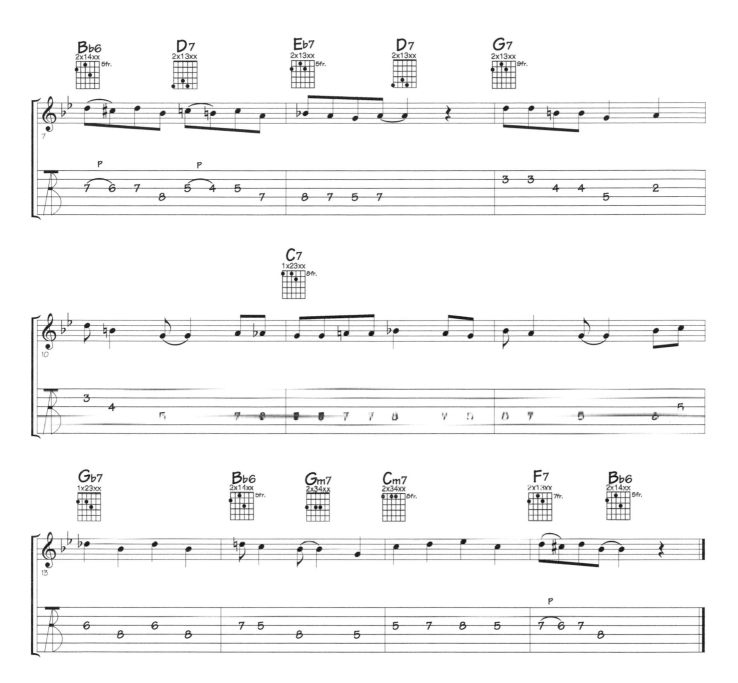

FIRST YOU PUT YOUR TWO KNEES CLOSE UP TIGHT
THEN YOU SWAY 'EM TO THE LEFT, THEN YOU SWAY 'EM TO THE RIGHT
STEP AROUND THE FLOOR KIND OF NICE AND LIGHT
THEN YOU TWIST AROUND AND TWIST AROUND WITH ALL YOUR MIGHT
STRETCH YOUR LOVIN' ARMS STRAIGHT OUT IN SPACE
THEN YOU DO THE EAGLE ROCK WITH STYLE AND GRACE
SWING YOUR FOOT WAY 'ROUND THEN BRING IT BACK
NOW THAT'S WHAT I CALL BALLIN' THE JACK

I AIN'T GOT NOBODY

Words by Roger Graham, music by Spencer Williams and Dave Peyton

The remaining tunes in this book are 32 bars long. "I Ain't Got Nobody" is more specifically in an AABA form, meaning that it begins with an eight-bar section (referred to as the A section), repeats that section (with some slight variations), proceeds to a contrasting eight-bar section or bridge (the B section), and concludes with a repeat of the original eight bars, possibly with another slight variation at the end.

David Lee Roth notwithstanding, the definitive version of this tune remains the one by Louis Prima, whose hit 1956 medley of "I Ain't Got Nobody" and "Just a Gigolo" (*Capitol Collectors Series: Louis Prima,* Capitol 94072) continues to turn up in Mafia movies on a regular basis. But if you can get by without the medley aspect, check out Benny Goodman's sublime small-group version on *Verve Jazz Masters 33: Benny Goodman* (Polygram 844410), Fats Waller's solo recording on *The Centennial Collection: Fats Waller* (RCA 59951), and Bob Wills and the Texas Playboys' western swing yodel-fest on *Historic Edition* (Columbia 55054). The Goodman and Waller versions are in the key of F.

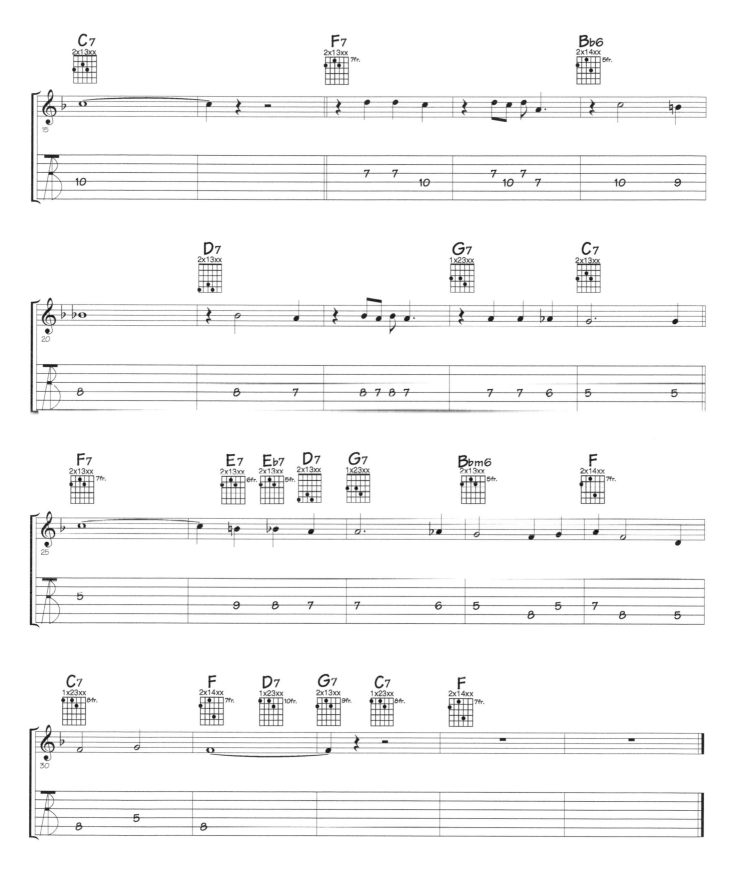

I AIN'T GOT NOBODY
AND NOBODY CARES FOR ME
AND I'M SAD AND LONELY
WON'T SOMEBODY COME AND TAKE A CHANCE WITH ME?
I'LL SING SWEET LOVE SONGS, HONEY
ALL THE TIME
IF YOU'LL COME AND BE MY
SWEET BABY MINE
'CAUSE I AIN'T GOT NOBODY
AND NOBODY CARES FOR ME

HINDUSTAN

Words and music by Oliver Wallace and Harold Weeks

While from the same era as the rest of these tunes, "Hindustan" did not really survive past the swing era, when it was popular with musicians like guitarist Eddie Condon and clarinetist Artie Shaw. Check out Condon's version on *Dr. Jazz: Volume 16* (Storyville 6061), and Shaw's on *Artie Shaw and His Orchestra: 1942–1945* (Classics Jazz 1242).

Perhaps the relaxed pace of the chord progression didn't give improvisers of the bebop era much to sink their teeth into, or maybe the lyrics about peacocks, camels, and temple bells didn't strike the same kind of timeless chord as sentiments like "I'll sing sweet love songs honey, all the time / If you'll come and be my sweet baby mine."

Just in case you were wondering (I know I was), "Hindustan" is an archaic name for the Indian subcontinent.

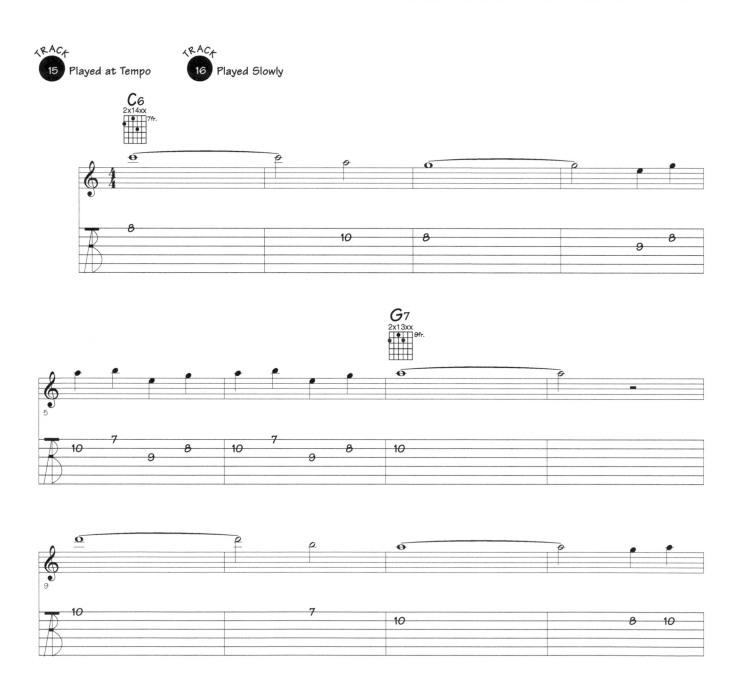

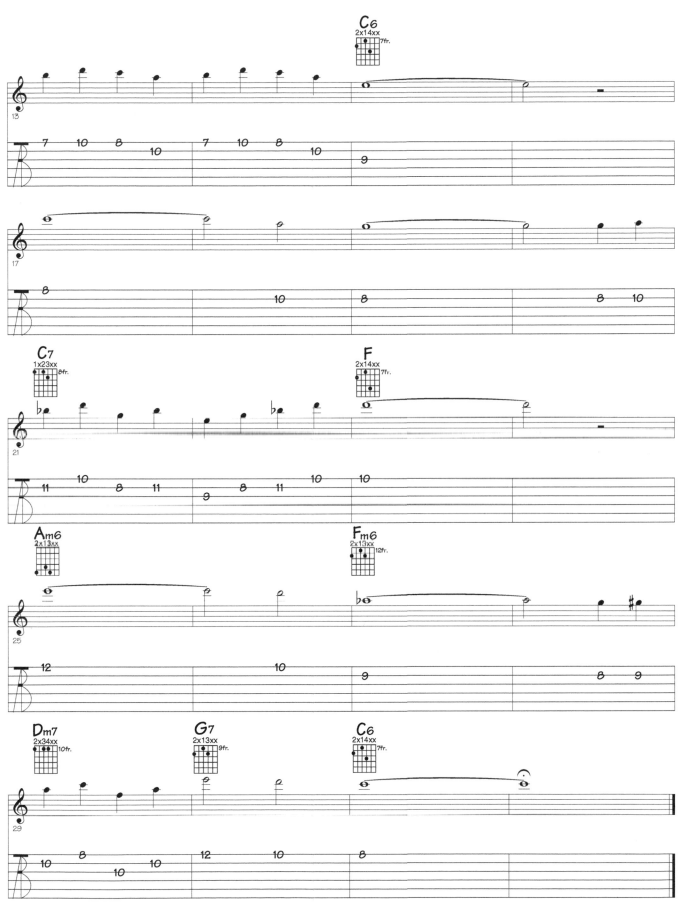

HINDUSTAN
WHERE WE STOP'D TO REST OUR TIRED CARAVAN
HINDUSTAN
WHERE THE PAINTED PEACOCK PROUDLY SPREAD HIS FAN
HINDUSTAN
WHERE THE PURPLE SUNBIRD FLASHED ACROSS THE SAND
HINDUSTAN
WHERE I MET HER AND THE WORLD BEGAN

AVALON

Words by Al Jolson and B. G. DeSylva, music by Vincent Rose

"**A**valon" has proved to be a much hardier tune than "Hindustan," despite the fact that it isn't even about a real place (in Celtic mythology, Avalon is the western island on which King Arthur and his colleagues are said to be lounging by the pool, sipping libations, and enjoying the afterlife). It was a big swing-era number for Benny Goodman and was also recorded by Coleman Hawkins, Teddy Wilson, and Jimmie Lunceford (check out

Swingsation: Jimmie Lunceford, GRP 9923) The modernists of the 1940s and '50s seem to have retained a certain affection for the song too, as evidenced by the recordings of pianists Elmo Hope and Red Garland and of reedmen Don Byas, Sonny Stitt, and Art Pepper. For a guitarcentric listen, check out versions by Chet Atkins (*Galloping Guitar: The Early Years*, Bear Family 15714) and Guy Van Duser (*American Fingerstyle Guitar*, Rounder 11533).

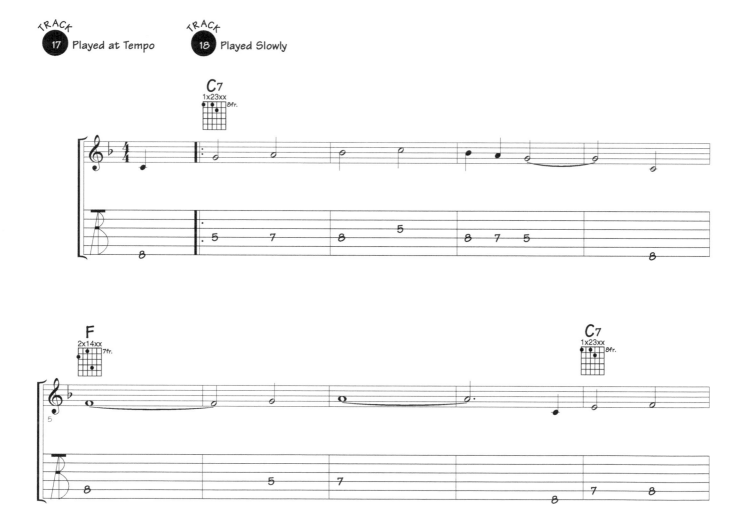

I FOUND MY LOVE IN AVALON
BESIDE THE BAY
I LEFT MY LOVE IN AVALON
AND SAIL'D AWAY
I DREAM OF HER AND AVALON
FROM DUSK TILL DAWN
AND SO I THINK I'LL TRAVEL ON
TO AVALON

POOR BUTTERFLY

Words by John L. Golden, music by Raymond Hubbell

There's usually a big difference between the way a song's chords are notated in the official published piano/vocal sheet music and the way jazz musicians play the chords in real life. Moreover, styles in chord accompaniment have evolved over time to the extent that, after a little listening, you can begin to peg the era in which a version of a popular song was recorded (or the era most admired by a group of contemporary musicians) by paying attention to how the chords are being played. The sheet music to "Poor Butterfly" calls for two measures of Eb7 in bars 1–2, 15–16, 17–18, and 29–30, but by the 1950s swing masters like Erroll Garner and Coleman Hawkins were replacing the first measure of Eb in each case with a measure of Bbm7, turning the two bars of the V chord into a bar of the ii7 chord and a bar of the V7 chord, or what bebop-schooled musicians

refer to simply as a ii–V. Check out Erroll Garner's version on *Long Ago and Far Away* (Columbia 40863) and Coleman Hawkins' on *At Ease with Coleman Hawkins* (Original Jazz Classics 181). Jazz guitarist Jim Hall plays "Poor Butterfly" on *Ballad Essentials* (Concord Jazz 4904).

The key to playing the melody is to stay basically in the third position (that is, use your index finger for the notes on the third fret, your middle finger for the notes on the fourth fret, and so on), and when you need to reach down for a note at the second fret, use your index finger for that note and for the one immediately after at the third fret. If you do this in the pickup measure, measure 4, measure 6, and so on, you can stay oriented by remaining in one position throughout the tune, and always have a finger available for the next note.

POOR BUTTERFLY, 'NEATH THE BLOSSOMS WAITING
POOR BUTTERFLY, FOR SHE LOVED HIM SO
THE MOMENTS PASS INTO HOURS, THE HOURS PASS INTO YEARS
AND AS SHE SMILES THROUGH HER TEARS, SHE MURMURS LOW
"THE MOON AND I KNOW THAT HE BE FAITHFUL
I'M SURE HE COME TO ME BY AND BY
BUT IF HE DON'T COME BACK THEN I NEVER SIGH OR CRY
I JUST MUST DIE," POOR BUTTERFLY

AFTER YOU'VE GONE

Words by Henry Creamer, music by Turner Layton

My initial exposure to this tune, as well as to "Limehouse Blues" and "Rose Room," was through the version by Django Reinhardt, Stéphane Grappelli, and the Quintet of the Hot Club of France (included on *Django Reinhardt, Volume 3: 1936–1937, Swing Guitars*, Naxos Jazz 812068). As the Hot Club version is pretty blazing, I was intrigued to come across a much more relaxed and reflective two-beat arrangement by the virtuoso solo pianist Art Tatum (*Classic Piano Solos: 1934–1937*, Decca Jazz 607). I therefore felt pretty set up when, a minute and half into

the record, Tatum paused, took a breath, and lit into a double-time version of the tune that ate the Hot Club's tempo for *pétit dejeuner*. The lesson I learned, however, is that "After You've Gone" sounds lovely at a more moderate tempo, which is how I've presented it here. On the CD I play through the tune twice to make it clear how the first and second endings work. For an even earlier jazz guitar take on this tune, give a listen to Eddie Lang's version on *The Quintessential Eddie Lang: 1925–1932* (Timeless 1043).

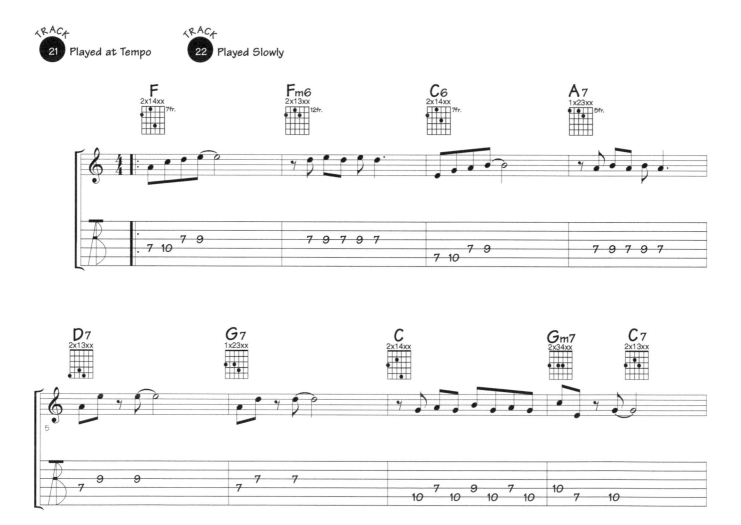

AFTER YOU'VE GONE AND LEFT ME CRYING
AFTER YOU'VE GONE THERE'S NO DENYING
YOU'LL FEEL BLUE, YOU'LL FEEL SAD
YOU'LL MISS THE DEAREST PAL YOU EVER HAD
THERE'LL COME A TIME, NOW DON'T FORGET IT
THERE'LL COME A TIME WHEN YOU'LL REGRET IT
SOMEDAY WHEN YOU GROW LONELY
YOUR HEART WILL BREAK LIKE MINE AND YOU'LL WANT ME ONLY
AFTER YOU'VE GONE, AFTER YOU'VE GONE AWAY

ROSE ROOM

Words by Harry Williams, music by Art Hickman

One of the first Charlie Christian solos I ever learned was the one on the Benny Goodman Sextet's version of "Rose Room" (heard on Charlie Christian, *Genius of the Electric Guitar*, Columbia 40846). The story goes that jazz impresario and Goodman manager John Hammond, Sr., brought the unknown Christian to the West Coast and, meeting with resistance from Goodman over the idea of Christian sitting in, had the band sneak the guitarist and his amplifier onto the stage during a break. When Goodman returned and spied Christian on the stand, he counted off

"Rose Room" in retaliation, figuring the peculiarly dressed hick from Oklahoma would be in tatters after one chorus. Instead, Christian tore through the changes, inspiring Goodman to go toe-to-toe with him on a series of choruses that reportedly went on for 45 minutes.

Other recordings of "Rose Room" can be found on Django Reinhardt, *Volume 3: 1936–1937, Swing Guitars*, Naxos Jazz 812068) and Jimmie Lunceford, *Stomp It Off* (GRP 608). The "Rose Room" chord progression is also the basis for Duke Ellington's tune "In a Mellow Tone."

IN SUNNY ROSELAND, WHERE SUMMER BREEZES ARE PLAYING
WHERE THE HONEY BEES ARE A-MAYING
THERE ALL THE ROSES ARE SWAYING
DANCING WHILE THE MEADOW BROOK FLOWS
THE MOON WHEN SHINING IS MORE THAN EVER DESIGNING
FOR 'TIS EVER THEN I AM PINING
PINING TO BE SWEETLY RECLINING
SOMEWHERE IN ROSELAND, BESIDE A BEAUTIFUL ROSE

LOOK FOR THE SILVER LINING

Words by Buddy DeSylva, music by Jerome Kern

My notion of how this tune ought to sound was formed by one of the first jazz records I ever heard, Joe Pass and Herb Ellis's *Jazz/Concord* (reissued with *Seven Come Eleven* as *Arrival*, Concord Jazz 2168). According to Ellis, their general strategy was for the more bop-oriented Pass to handle the chords on the way into the tune, while the more swing-inspired Ellis took the melody. But what's most exhilarating about their performance is the moment when they drop the solo/backup scheme of things entirely, along with the rhythm section, and embark on a simultaneous improvisation, weaving in and out of each other's lines and wailing like a space-age version of Carl Kress and Dick McDonough. (Kress and McDonaugh recorded a handful of jazz duets in the 1930s that have been anthologized, along with work by Lonnie Johnson and Eddie Lang and others,

on *Pioneers of the Jazz Guitar*, Yazoo 1057. Indispensable listening if you like that sort of thing.)

While Pass and Ellis do "Look for the Silver Lining" in the original key of E♭, I've presented it in B♭ to facilitate moves like the climbing/descending voicings in measures 6–7. Measure 25 really calls for an Em7♭5, but since the ♭5 note of the chord, A♮, would be played on the second string (see the chord section of the introductory notes on "The Rhythm Style"), our three-string Em7 voicing works as a kind of shorthand for the full chord.

Trumpeter/vocalist Chet Baker performs this song on *Chet Baker in Milan* (Original Jazz Classics 370), and a version by saxophonist Paul Desmond can be heard on the curiously titled *Paul Desmond Quintet Plus the Paul Desmond Quartet* (Original Jazz Classics 712).

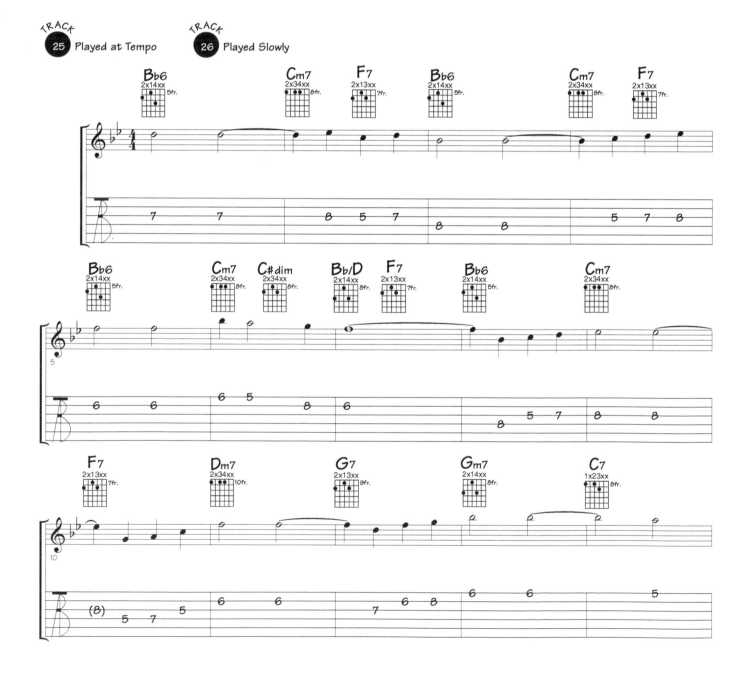

LOOK FOR THE SILVER LINING
WHENE'ER A CLOUD APPEARS IN THE SKY
REMEMBER SOMEWHERE THE SUN IS SHINING
AND SO THE RIGHT THING TO DO IS MAKE IT SHINE FOR YOU
A HEART FULL OF JOY AND GLADNESS
WILL ALWAYS BANISH SADNESS AND STRIFE
SO ALWAYS LOOK FOR THE SILVER LINING
AND TRY TO FIND THE SUNNY SIDE OF LIFE

INDIANA

Words by Ballard MacDonald, music by James F. Hanley

"Indiana" was already the kind of tune swing musicians liked to play at a knuckle-busting clip when bebop alto saxophonist Charlie Parker used the song's chord changes as the basis for his tune "Donna Lee." Both tunes survived the process and remain somewhat linked as a result—when Barry Harris, a devoted bopper, recorded "Indiana" on *Chasin' the Bird* (Original Jazz Classics 872), the tempo, phrasing, and chord voicings all could have dropped right out of "Donna Lee." More swing-oriented recordings of "Indiana" can be heard on Scott Hamilton's CD *From the Beginning* (Concord Jazz 2117) and on Barney Kessel's *To Swing or Not to Swing: Vol. 3* (Original Jazz Classics 317).

Like all of the 32-bar bar tunes in this book except "I Ain't Got Nobody," "Indiana" is an ABAC form. That is, bars 1–8 make up the A section, which is immediately followed by an answering eight bars, or B section. Bars 17–24, the second A section, are a variation on the first eight bars, and the concluding eight bars, different from everything else so far, make up the C section. If the Em in measures 23, 25, and 27 is too much of a stretch, you can substitute an Em7 voicing (with your pinkie at the seventh fret of the third string).

TRACK 27 Played at Tempo   TRACK 28 Played Slowly

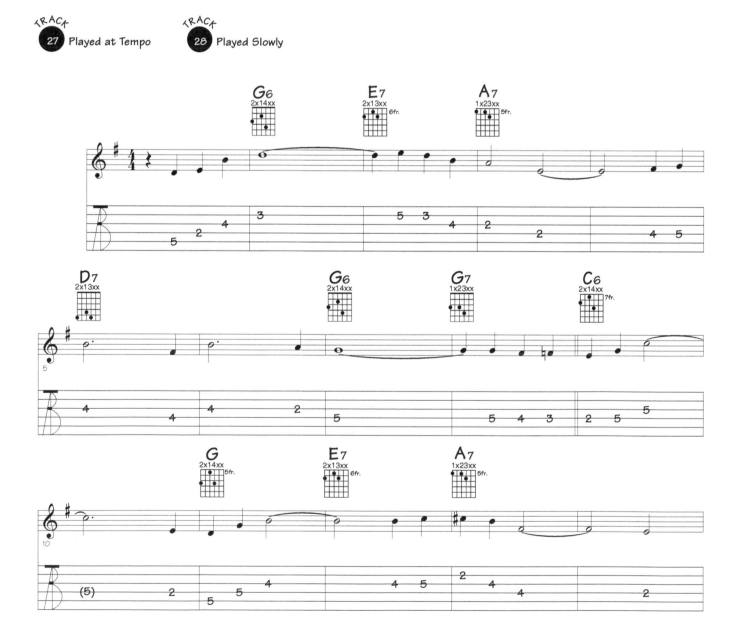

BACK HOME AGAIN IN INDIANA
AND IT SEEMS THAT I CAN SEE
THE GLEAMING CANDLELIGHT STILL SHINING BRIGHT
THROUGH THE SYCAMORES FOR ME
THE NEW MOWN HAY SENDS ALL ITS FRAGRANCE
FROM THE FIELDS I USED TO ROAM
WHEN I DREAM ABOUT THE MOONLIGHT ON THE WABASH
THEN I LONG FOR MY INDIANA HOME

LIMEHOUSE BLUES

Words by Douglas Furber, music by Philip Braham

In 1922 songs often talked about having one kind of blues or another without necessarily embodying the blues musically. "Limehouse Blues" is not a 12-bar blues per se, but the opening D♭7, or IV7 in the song's key of A♭, sets up a bluesier feel than a regular major IV chord would.

Part of London's East End, Limehouse was home to that city's Chinatown at the turn of the 20th century. "Limehouse Blues" told a story of lost love and broken promises in what today would be considered scathingly racist terms, but as with many standards, most of the damage was done in the rarely recalled introductory verse, and since the 1920s

vocal versions of the song have been far outnumbered by instrumental renditions anyway.

This tune has remained popular with more contemporary artists, so you may want to check out recent versions by David Grisman and Mike Auldridge (*Tone Poems III*, Acoustic Disc 42) or Frank Vignola (*Blues for a Gypsy*, Acoustic Disc 43). For an earlier jazz guitar version, check out the work of Oscar Alemán, "the Argentinian Django," on *Swing Guitar Masterpieces* (Acoustic Disc 29), and for yet more swing-era virtuosity, there's always Art Tatum (*At the Piano*, GNP/Crescendo 9025).

OH LIMEHOUSE KID, OH, OH, OH LIMEHOUSE KID
GOING THE WAY THAT THE REST OF THEM DID
POOR BROKEN BLOSSOM AND NOBODY'S CHILD
HAUNTING AND TAUNTING YOU'RE JUST KIND OF WILD, OH, OH
OH LIMEHOUSE BLUES, I'VE THE REAL LIMEHOUSE BLUES
CAN'T SEEM TO SHAKE OFF THOSE SAD CHINA BLUES
RINGS ON YOUR FINGERS AND TEARS FOR YOUR CROWN
THAT IS THE STORY OF OLD CHINATOWN

TILL THE CLOUDS ROLL BY

Words by P. G. Wodehouse, music by Jerome Kern

I lifted—er, drew creative inspiration—from nylon-string jazz guitarist Charlie Byrd's version (*Du Hot Club de Concord*, Concord Jazz 4674) for this arrangement of the chord changes. The original music calls for simply rocking between I and V7 for a bar apiece over the first six bars; the reharmonization here is a typical swing-era strategy for creating motion while staying well within the key of the song. The result is an accompaniment that shifts chord voicings every two beats wherever possible.

This tune, despite its its lovely, wistful melody, doesn't seem to be in wide circulation, and as such gets my vote for

Song in This Book Most Deserving of Wider Recognition. The lyrics were written by P. G. Wodehouse, creator of Jeeves and Bertie Wooster, and they make use of the same kind of whimsical, mock-tragic language that might be heard from one of his short story characters. In the 1920s, Wodehouse was a frequent collaborator with composer Jerome Kern, whose later work includes "Smoke Gets in Your Eyes," "A Fine Romance," and "All the Things You Are." Kern also collaborated with Buddy DeSylva in 1920 on "Look for the Silver Lining."

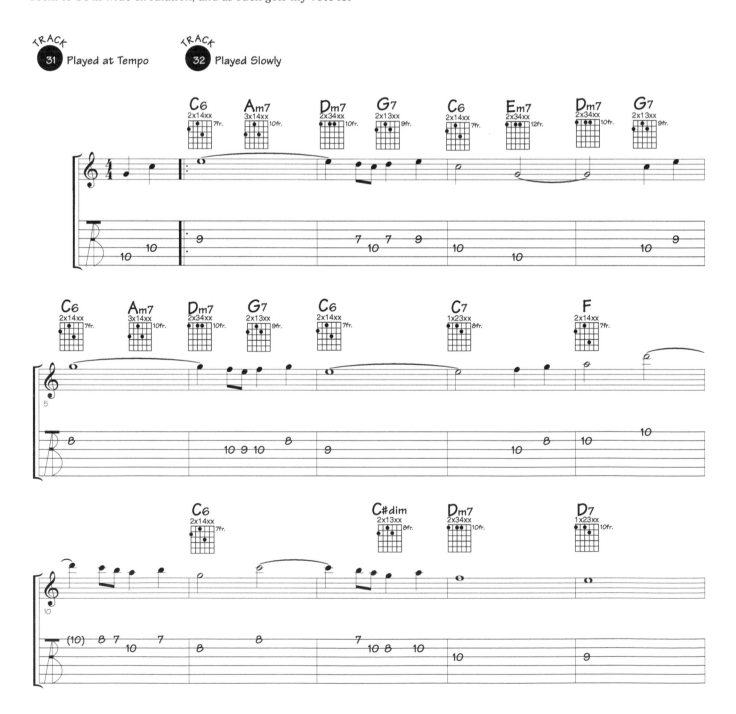

OH THE RAIN COMES A PITTER, PATTER
AND I'D LIKE TO BE SAFE IN BED
SKIES ARE WEEPING, WHILE THE WORLD IS SLEEPING
TROUBLE HEAPING ON OUR HEAD
IT IS VAIN TO REMAIN AND CHATTER
AND TO WAIT FOR A CLEARER SKY
HELTER SKELTER I MUST FLY FOR SHELTER
TILL THE CLOUDS ROLL BY

ABOUT THE AUTHOR

David Hamburger is the the author of several books, including *The Acoustic Guitar Method, Acoustic Guitar Slide Basics,* and *Beginning Blues Guitar.* A contributing editor to *Acoustic Guitar,* he has written dozens of magazine lessons on everything from swing improvisation, flatpicking, and music theory to fingerstyle blues, slide guitar, and open tunings. For several years, his classes on swing guitar and "Blue Note Blues" have been among the most popular offerings at the National Guitar Workshop, where he has also co-led seminars with Duke Robillard on swing and blues styles.

Hamburger has released three solo CDs, toured with Joan Baez, and spent a season playing guitar on the Food Network show *Emeril Live,* where he was better known to the audience as C. F. Steaks. He currently lives in Austin, Texas, where he plays Dobro with the bluegrass band the Grassy Knoll Boys and fronts the acoustic blues quintet Beaumont Lagrange. For a discography and performance schedule, visit www.davidhamburger.com.

ACKNOWLEDGMENTS

Thanks to Duke Robillard for a hands-on education in the Freddie Green style (and to Mickey Baker for *Mickey Baker's Jazz Guitar*); to John Good for the jazz library at the Independent Free State of 51 Park Place, Middletown, Connecticut, circa 1985–86; and to Paul Hamburger, the first pianist I ever met who played show tunes, and Eddie Hamburger, who was presumably the second. Thanks also to Rob Lancefield for tackling my questions about orientalism and jazz. And special thanks to Catherine Berry, who would have been OK with it if writing this book had involved moments of rending my garments and questioning all that I hold dear, but was no doubt quite pleased that it did not.

STRING LETTER PUBLISHING

presents

The Acoustic Guitar Method
by David Hamburger

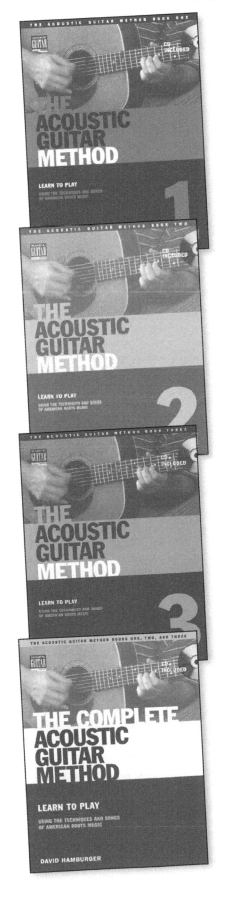

BOOK 1

We're proud to present the first in a series of beginning method books that uses
traditional American music to teach authentic techniques and songs. From the folk, blues, and old-time
music of yesterday have come the rock, country, and jazz of today. Now you can begin understanding,
playing, and enjoying these essential traditions and styles on the instrument that truly represents American
music: the acoustic guitar. Working in both tablature and standard notation, you'll learn how to find notes
on the fingerboard, a variety of basic chords and strums, country backup basics, waltz time, and melodies
with half notes and rests. When you're done with this method series, you'll know dozens of the tunes that
form the backbone of American music and be able to play them using a variety of flatpicking and
fingerpicking techniques. Songs: Man of Constant Sorrow • Columbus Stockade Blues • Careless Love •
Get Along Home, Cindy • Sally Goodin • Ida Red • Darling Corey • Hot Corn, Cold Corn • East Virginia
Blues • In the Pines • Banks of the Ohio • Scarborough Fair • Shady Grove.
_____00695648 Book/CD Pack..$9.95

BOOK 2

Learn how to alternate the bass notes to a country backup pattern, how to connect
chords with some classic bass runs, and how to play your first fingerpicking patterns. You'll find out what
makes a major scale work and what blues notes do to a melody, all while learning more notes on the
fingerboard and more great songs from the American roots repertoire – especially from the blues
tradition. Songs include: Columbus Stockade Blues • Frankie and Johnny • The Girl I Left Behind Me •
Way Downtown • and more.
_____00695649 Book/CD Pack..$9.95

BOOK 3

Working in both tablature and standard notation, you'll continue to expand your collection
of chords by learning songs in various keys as well as different kinds of picking patterns. When you're
done with this method series, you'll know dozens of the tunes that form the backbone of American music
and be able to play them using a variety of flatpicking and fingerpicking techniques. Book Three
introduces 12 new songs from the blues, folk, country, and bluegrass traditions.
_____00695666 Book/CD Pack..$9.95

COMPLETE EDITION

Get all three method book/CD packs in The Acoustic Guitar Method in one money-saving
volume.
_____00695667 Book/CD Pack..$24.95

Prices, contents, and availability subject to change without notice.

FOR MORE INFORMATION, SEE YOUR LOCAL MUSIC DEALER,
OR WRITE TO:

HAL•LEONARD®
CORPORATION
7777 W. BLUEMOUND RD. P.O. BOX 13819 MILWAUKEE, WI 53213

Visit Hal Leonard Online at **www.halleonard.com**
Acoustic Guitar Central at **www.acousticguitar.com**

Hal Leonard Presents Guitar Instruction from

S T R I N G   L E T T E R   P U B L I S H I N G

The accompanying CDs in these book/CD packs feature all examples played slowly and up to tempo. All books are part of the *Acoustic Guitar Private Lessons* series.

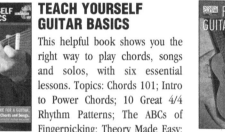

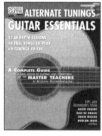